J
976.4   **Thompson, Kathleen**
T   **Texas**

TEXAS

Copyright © 1986 Raintree Publishers Inc.

All rights reserved. No part of this book may be reproduced
or utilized in any form or by any means, electronic or mechanical,
including photocopying, recording or by any information storage
and retrieval system, without permission in writing from the
Publisher. Inquiries should be addressed to Raintree Publishers Inc.
330 East Kilbourn Avenue, Milwaukee, Wisconsin 53202.

A Turner Educational Services, Inc. book. Based on the Portrait
of America television series created by R.E. (Ted) Turner.

Library of Congress Number: 85-9980

1234567890   908988878685

Library of Congress Cataloging in Publication Data

Thompson, Kathleen.
  Texas.

  (Portrait of America)
  "A Turner book."
  Summary: Discusses the history, economy, culture,
and future of Texas. Also includes a state
chronology, pertinent statistics, and maps.
  1. Texas—Juvenile literature. [1. Texas]
I. Title. II. Series: Thompson, Kathleen. Portrait of
America.
F386.3.T46 1985   976.4   85-9980
ISBN 0-86514-445-1 (lib. bdg.)
ISBN 0-86514-520-2 (softcover)

Cover Photo: Grant Heilman, Grant Heilman Photography

★ ★ ★ ★ ★
Portrait of AMERICA

TEXAS

Kathleen Thompson

Photographs from Portrait of America programs
courtesy of Turner Program Services, Inc.

A TURNER BOOK
RAINTREE PUBLISHERS

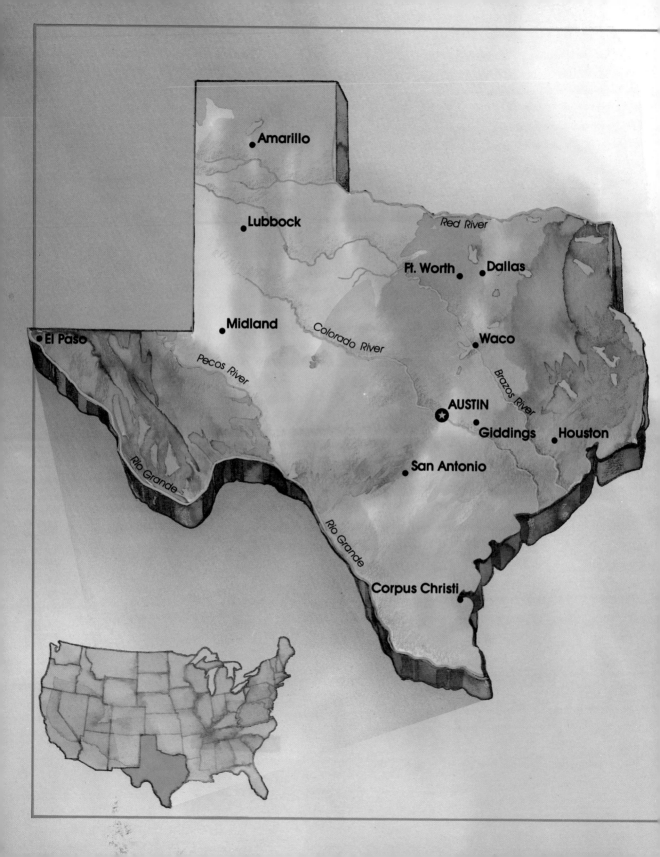

CONTENTS

Introduction

Texas, the Lone Star State.

"I've traveled a great deal and when people ask me, 'Well, where're you from?' I've never, not once, said 'I'm from the United States.' I say, 'I'm from Texas.'"

Texas: cowboys, moon rockets, oil wells, land.

"If we was to meet a bunch of the old cowpunchers . . . I think we'd get along real good. We're made out of the same stuff, I think."

Texas is big. Big enough for three or four states. Big enough to hold a lot of different people and a lot of different ways of life. But, in a way, Texas is more the same than you'd think. There's a spirit that comes from being on the frontier—of the country, of space, of the future. Texans are used to breaking new ground.

The frontier spirit is one of courage, of determination, of recklessness. . . . You'll find it all on the plains and in the cities of Texas.

From the Apaches to Apollo 11

The population of Texas was around 30,000 at the time. The land was covered with small farms, each producing enough for its own needs and maybe a little over. Many of the small local governments had formed a confederacy that preserved peace and order on a larger scale.

The time was the 1400s and those 30,000 people were American Indians.

In the eastern part of what is now Texas were the Caddo Indians. Some of these tribes, including the Nacogdoches, Nasoni, and Neche, were part of the Hasinai Confederacy. Other tribes lived along the coast of Texas. They included the Arkokisa, Attacapa, Karankawa, and others. In south Texas were the Coahuiltecan Indians.

In the LBJ National Historic Park, farm life in the early 1900s is recreated.

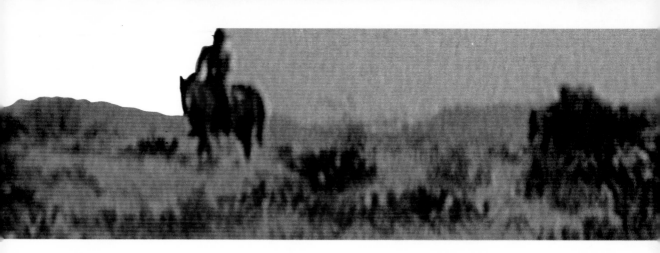

To the west were the Lipan Apaches, and the Comanche and Tonkawa Indians lived on the plains of the north central part of Texas.

It wasn't entirely peaceful. The quiet farmers of the east feared the fiercer Apaches of the west. But it was a civilization that worked in the vast lands of Texas.

Then, in the early 1500s Spanish explorers came into the area looking for gold. And the land was changed forever.

In 1519, the Spanish governor of Jamaica sent an explorer, Alonso Álvarez de Piñeda, to explore the coast around the Gulf of Mexico. They were probably the first Europeans to enter Texas. They made maps of the region and reported back.

In 1528, a group of Spanish explorers was shipwrecked on the coast of Texas. Four of the men survived the wreck and traveled west for eight years. The leader of the group was Alvar Núñez Cabeza de Vaca. One of the others, a man named Estevanico—or Estéban—later guided explorers into New Mexico. It was this group that, when they reached a Spanish settlement near the west coast of Mexico, brought back stories of golden cities and great wealth.

Many more Spanish explorers followed, looking for these fabled cities, the Seven Cities of Cibola. In 1541, Francisco Vásquez de Coronado passed through Texas on his search for gold, but all he found were farms and villages and adobe houses.

The Spanish never found the golden cities, but they did find Texas. And they claimed it for their own. In 1682, Roman Catho-

lic missionaries built the first missions in Texas, near what is now El Paso.

But the Spanish were not the only Europeans who were interested in this great section of the Southwest. In 1685, a Frenchman named Robert Cavelier, Sieur de la Salle, came to Texas by mistake. He meant to start a colony at the mouth of the Mississippi River. It was probably a storm that blew him to the coast of Texas instead. But he decided to make the best of it and started a colony a little ways inland. He named it Fort Saint Louis. Then he started making trips west. Like the Spanish, he was looking for silver and gold. In 1687, La Salle was killed by one of his own men and the others in the group died soon after. Sickness took some of them. Others were killed by Indians who were try-

During the first 100 years of Texas's settlement, missions dotted the vast Texas landscape.

ing to protect their land from the European explorers.

The Spanish continued to send explorers and missionaries into Texas. Missions were built all over the central, eastern, and southwestern areas of what is now Texas. And forts were built to protect the missions. A Spanish government was set up. But by 1793, after more than a hundred years of missions and explorations, there were still only 7,000 European settlers in Texas.

It was about that time that the United States entered the pic-

ture. In 1803, the United States bought the Louisiana Territory from France and claimed all the territory as far south as the Rio Grande River. In 1819, a treaty was made. United States territory was to stop at the Sabine and Red rivers.

But a long history of conflict remained for Texas. Mexico broke away from Spain in 1821, and Texas became part of the Empire of Mexico.

The Alamo (below) was the site of a famous battle in which a group of Texas rebels—including Davy Crockett (shown in the painting)—were defeated.

The Mexican government freely granted permission for Americans to settle in Texas. The first American colony was founded by Stephen Austin. His father, Moses Austin, had wanted to bring settlers into Texas, but he had died before he could carry out his plan. So his son took over and brought 300 families to Texas.

The Austin colony grew and grew. New land grants were issued by the Mexican government. Stephen Austin created San Felipe de Austin in what is now Austin County, and the colony was governed from there.

There were other American colonies too, all founded with the permission of the Mexican government. But then Mexico began to get worried. Between 1821 and 1836, the numbers of settlers in Texas—mostly Americans—grew to around 30,000. The Mexican government refused permission for any more Americans to come into Texas.

From that point, there was more and more trouble between the American settlers and the Mexican government. And then in 1834, General Antonio López de Santa Anna overthrew Mexico's constitutional government and made himself dictator. The next year, the Americans in Texas began to fight for freedom from Mexico.

In 1835, Texas leaders formed a temporary government. They sent out troops to attack San Antonio and they won. Then Santa Anna formed a large army and marched on San Antonio.

They called that the battle of the Alamo.

The Texas rebels in San Antonio took over an old Spanish mission called the Alamo. From behind its walls, they fought Santa Anna's army. The rebels —Davy Crockett, Jim Bowie, William Travis, and others— held out for ten days. On the eleventh day, March 6, 1836, the Alamo fell. All its defenders had been killed in the battle.

But in the meantime, Texas leaders had met at Washington-on-the-Brazos and declared their independence from Mexico. They chose David G. Burnet as temporary president and Sam Houston as commander of the Army.

Santa Anna wasn't about to give up, however. At Goliad, on

March 27, he had more than 330 Texas prisoners shot to death. The Texas army kept fighting. Their battle cries were "Remember the Alamo" and "Remember Goliad." On April 21, Sam Houston's army took the much larger Mexican army by surprise. They captured General Santa Anna and defeated his forces. Texas was now an independent country.

But it was a country with problems. For one thing, it didn't have any money. Also, Mexican raids continued. And the Indians of Texas had not given up on their land. In Texas's first national election, the people chose Sam Houston as president and voted to join the United States.

But not everyone wanted Texas to be part of the United States. The Northern states in the Union objected because Texas allowed slavery. France and Great Britian didn't want Texas to join the Union because they were afraid it would help the United States to take over the entire Southwest. It took ten years for the republic of Texas to become the state of Texas. But in December of 1845, Texas was voted the twenty-eighth

Portrait of America

A large Texas ranch (above) contrasts with a small farm (right). This farm, in central Texas, uses a windmill for power to pump water.

state by a joint resolution of both houses of Congress. J. Pinckney Henderson, a Democrat, became the first governor.

All the time, the population of Texas was growing. In 1839, Texas had passed a very important law. It was a homestead exemption act. This law stated that no one could lose a farm simply for being unable to pay

Texas Tourist Development Agency, Photo by Michael Murphy

debts. This gave the small farmers of Texas a much better chance to make it on the land.

After Texas joined the union, Mexico and the United States went to war. After two years of fighting, the Mexican forces surrendered. In 1848, a treaty was signed. Mexico gave up its claim to Texas and all other southwestern lands.

Now, Texas claimed that most of that land should be part of its state. In 1850, the United States government paid the state of Texas $10 million for its claims, and Texas used the money to pay some of its debts.

And Texas continued to grow. More settlers came into the state and pushed the frontier farther west.

15

Then came the Civil War. After waiting so long to become a part of the United States, Texas was one of the states that seceded from the Union. In March 1861, Texas joined the Confederate States of America.

Large parts of Texas did not agree with this decision. Governor Sam Houston refused to support the Confederacy and was put out of office.

Still, 50,000 Texans fought on the Confederate side in the war. And huge amounts of supplies went from Texas to the rest of the Confederacy. More than a month after the Civil War ended, there was a battle at Palmito Hill, near the mouth of the Rio

During the 1880s, railroads, with trains like the one at the left, began to cross the cattle land of Texas.

Texas Tourist Development Agency, Photo by Richard Reynolds

violence against blacks broke out. The Ku Klux Klan became powerful. During Reconstruction, Texas was ruled by a military government, a governor appointed by the federal government, and three governors elected by the Northern sympathizers called Radicals. In 1870, Texas was readmitted to the United States.

After the Civil War, big cattle drives began from Texas to the railroad centers in Kansas and Missouri. Those were the golden days of the cowboy. Thousands of men looking for work in the out-of-doors, who were not afraid of hardship and danger, joined the drives.

In western Texas, Indians still fought to keep their lands, but by 1880, they had lost. Cattlemen moved into the Panhandle and the plains in the west.

Then came the railroads. The great cattle drives were over. They had lasted only about twenty years, but they had left a lasting mark on the American imagination.

During this time, settlers had

Grande. The soldiers hadn't heard the war was over.

The time after the Civil War—Reconstruction—was a terrible time all over the United States. In Texas, a group of people sympathetic to the Union's cause came into power in state government. But Southern sympathizers were angry. Lawlessness and

been protected by the Texas Rangers. Organized in 1835, the rangers patrolled the frontier, fighting Indians and the bandits who tried to rob and kill ranchers and farmers.

And then, suddenly, there was oil.

The Spindletop oil field was discovered in 1901 near Beaumont. The boom was on. Soon there were black derricks rising all over the flat land of Texas. The riches the Spanish explorers had dreamed about were there after all. Not gold, but the precious black liquid.

With the oil came the refineries. And big manufacturing plants. The harbors along the coast were now filled with ships for taking oil to the world. Workers came from the farms and ranches to the oil fields.

After the United States entered the first World War, military training camps were set up in many parts of Texas. In the 1920s, important improvements

Oil was first discovered in Texas in 1866. By 1920 oil fields with derricks like those in the two upper photographs had sprung up all over Texas. A present-day pump is shown at the left.

were made in education and the prison system. In 1925, Texas elected a woman governor. She was Miriam A. "Ma" Ferguson. Only one other state, Wyoming, had ever elected a woman to this high office.

After the second World War, Texas became more involved in manufacturing. The new factories took more workers out of the rural areas and brought them to the cities. Texas was changing very quickly.

In the 1950s and 1960s Texas faced many of the same problems that were being dealt with in other states. There were separate schools for black children and for white children. In 1954, the Supreme Court of the United States ruled that this segregation was against the constitution.

In 1962, the National Aeronautics and Space Administration (NASA) built a Manned Spacecraft Center near Houston. It was from this center that the Apollo 11 flight was directed. Houston scientists and engineers, along with the rest of NASA, had put an astronaut on the moon.

Above is the skyline of Houston. At the right (below) is President John F. Kennedy and Jacqueline Kennedy in Dallas on the day the president was assassinated.

One of the tragic moments in American history happened in Dallas in 1963. President John F. Kennedy was killed as he passed the Texas School Book Depository. The man accused of shooting him, Lee Harvey Oswald, was shot two days later by a nightclub owner, Jack Ruby. Lyndon B. Johnson, Kennedy's vice-president, became president, the first Southerner to become president of the United States since the Civil War.

The Manned Spacecraft Center in Houston was renamed the Lyndon B. Johnson Space Center in 1973. Because of it, southeastern Texas is a major center for space research.

Today, Texas has a population of over fourteen million. The small Indian farms are gone. So are most of the big cattle ranches. Walking the streets of a Texas city, you will still see cowboy hats and boots. But Texas stands squarely in the modern world.

The Cowboy

There have been cowboys in lots of places, from the pampas of Brazil and Argentine to the hills of Wyoming. And yet, when you think of cowboys, you often think of Texas.

"The cowboy is still the great American hero: independent, adventurous, totally self-sufficient. There aren't as many cowboys—real true cowboys—as there used to be."

The great years of the Texas cattle drives were from about 1865 to about 1880. Then the railroads came to Texas and things changed. But there were still the roundups. There was still a place for the cowboy.

"When I was a young fellow—I believe this is the truth—if you carried a canteen on your saddle horn, you were a sissy. So none of us did. If we had to go all day without water, okay. Or if we hit a muddied water hole we drank from that."

A cowboy's life was hard and dangerous. But that was part of what drew people to it. The United States had, from the very beginning, been a place for people who wanted to be close to the land, who dreamed, not of the bright lights and the big cities, but of wilderness. Then, as the trails were blazed and the wild lands tamed, there was less room for the woodsman, the mountain man, the explorer.

There was still room for the cowboy. In Texas, there *is* still room for the cowboy.

"Well, it's not only an occupation; it's a way of life. It's not any nine-to-five job. It's daylight to dark, and then a lot of times it lasts after the sun goes down. It's something that really takes your heart, and unless you've had that love for it, you never can really know what it means."

At the right is a Texas rancher. Below is a view of the Chihuahua Desert.

Texas Tourist Development Agency, Photo by Richard Reynolds

On the 0-6 Ranch in west Texas, cowboys still do the roundup just about the way it was done in the 1800s. It's a tradition.

"We could use helicopters, I suppose, but we're all in it for the way of life. We're not in it for getting the job done a little quicker or a little easier. We all enjoy what we're doing. This ranch has always been operated and managed by cow people that are interested in running livestock and handling them in a traditional manner, managing the ranch so that there'll always be a supply of grass here."

Portrait of America

Diane Lacey is shown against an aerial view of San Antonio.

One thing that's a little unusual on the 0-6 is that Diane Lacey is a woman who works the roundup and runs the family ranch with her husband, Chris.

"I'm from San Antonio, and I just lived the big-city life. I was used to traffic and parties and society and all that, you know. And out here, it just doesn't seem that important to me anymore. Your values change. I think the main thing about living out like this is that you have to come in contact with the real basics of life."

There aren't many ranches like the 0-6. There aren't many places like west Texas. Today there are urban cowboys and rhinestone cowboys and lots of people in ten gallon hats and tall boots who will never get closer to a horse—or a cow—than the mechanical bull in a country bar. But the cowboy lives on, in our imaginations and on the plains of Texas.

"Oh, yeah, there'll always be cowboys. As long as there's cattle and people eat beef, there'll be cowboys."

Portrait of America

Another Kind of Oil Town

Everybody knows about Texas oil and Texas oil millionaires. They're big, brash, and showy. And they don't care who knows it.

"A fella, a friend of mine, he said, 'I just love being new rich because I don't

Oil wells and money but a small town feeling . . . typify the city of Giddings.

Shelby Scharine

have any relatives . . . or bloodlines that I have to worry about offending.' Whatever I do, I do on my own, you know, I'm blazing a trail."

But there are all kinds of oil millionaires in Texas. And some of them live in Giddings, a small town in central Texas. The people in Giddings are the children and grandchildren, many of them, of the Wendish farmers who came here to escape religious persecution in Germany. Their faith and their values have had a lot to do with how they have dealt with the miracle of oil.

"What you're looking at there is one hundred percent oil. This is called the Giddings honey-colored oil. Most of the good wells in Giddings, the oil looks just like that. It's what puts money in the bank."

With all that money in the bank, Giddings remains a small town with a small town feeling. And the people . . .

"Very few people talk about it, because they're not sure their wealth is going to stay. But there are a lot of people here that are rich from oil. But a lot of people still live the way they lived before."

The barber still cuts hair.

"It didn't change things for me. I kept on workin'. And I'm still trying to work."

The farmer still works his farm.

"We didn't realize that it was oil under here, and the Lord done give the wisdom to pull it out of here. But, I don't think it changed my spirit any. And I'm not proud and haughty, and I kind of feel like . . . this was a humble well. And I always felt like, 'Stay humble with the Lord.'"

Of course, things have changed. Myrtle Collins had a tiny farm and had to use food stamps to help out. She didn't like doing it. Now she has some of the things her mother always wanted.

"I used to hear my mother say, 'If I ever get hold of any money, I'm going to sure get me a nice fence, because that one just looks terrible.' That was the first thing I did—put a fence around here. And then after I got the house, I had it done. She always talked about having paneling. So I had paneling put from the front to the back, all over it just like she wanted. Then I had it painted, new ceiling lights, everything she wanted. . . . And when I got through with everything I just come outside and looked all around. I said, 'Well, Mama, I don't know where you are, but wherever it is, here it is. I got it! And I hope you can see it, you know.'"

Two States
for the Price of One

If you took a map of Texas and drew a line from the top of the state to the bottom, just west of Dallas, you'd be dividing it into two very different areas.

On one side of the line, to the east, you'd find most of the big industrial cities. You'd also find cotton and rice farms, pecan groves, forests. On the western side, you'd find cotton, too. But this is cattle, oil, and wheat country, for the most part.

The line is a natural one. To the east, there's water. And water means rich farm land. It's also necessary for factories and cities. To the west, the land makes up for its lack of water with rich mineral resources and vast grasslands for cattle.

More than half of the value of goods produced in Texas

A view of Big Bend National Park with the Chisos Mountains in the background.

comes from manufacturing. The chief manufactured products are chemicals, nonelectric machinery, petroleum and coal products, and food products. That may seem surprising. Most of us probably think only of oil and cattle when we think of Texas. But the fact is, Texas is one of the leading manufacturing states in the country.

Then, about one-third of the goods produced by Texas are mineral. That includes oil, Texas's most valuable mineral. About a billion barrels of crude oil come out of Texas every year.

Natural gas is the second most

valuable Texas mineral. The state produces about 40 percent of all the natural gas that comes out of the United States every year. And there are other important minerals in Texas—sulfur, salt, graphite and magnesium, helium, asphalt, fluorspar, many kinds of clay, granite, gypsum,

coal, and other minerals also come from Texas.

Texas is a leading agricultural state, too. It has more farms than any other state, about 159,000.

Cattle is the largest agricultural product. With its large areas of grassland and winters mild enough for cattle to graze the year around, Texas leads all states in beef cattle production.

The biggest crop raised in Texas is cotton, followed by sorghum grain. But there's a lot of rice grown in the state, too. And wheat. And corn, cottonseed, hay, oats, soybeans, sugar beets, and sugarcane. And that's only the beginning.

Texas is also an important producer of vegetables and fruit. It's a leader in pecan and peanut production. And Texas raises more sheep than any other state.

Texas also produces more electricity than any other state. So, whether you want to make a pecan pie or blow dry your hair, Texas is the place to do it.

Texas leads the nation in the production of beef cattle (far left) and sheep (left).

Texas Tourist Development Agency, Photo by Michael Murphy

N. E. Upshaw,
the patriarch of the
Upshaw family.

The Upshaws of East Texas

"My Daddy was an all-around man. He could build wagons and make anything out of wood, shingles, boards, and then he'd build fish traps and get fish off of that, and alligators and turtles. Alligator hide was worth lots of money. Make shoes. You seen them alligator shoes? Did you see all them knots on them? That was way back there in his early days. That was way before my time, but I heard him talking about it all the time during my early life."

After the Civil War, thousands of southerners came to east Texas. Here you don't see the big, dry plains of the west. There are pine woods and fertile land. Here, 22,000 black people from the south made the dream of owning their own land come true.

The Upshaws were one of those families. There were three boys, sons of Rachel Upshaw.

"And their names were Felix, Jim, and Gus. And my father, N.E., here, is Gus's son. And so they had to come into

this wilderness of a land and carve out a place, a community, a home by first felling the trees. And this is how the community started, by just sheer strength and bulldog tenacity. The Upshaws were strong people. . . . If they'd been small people they probably could not have survived in the wilderness area."

The Upshaws have scattered now. But they return to Nacogdoches County to remember their past. It's important to them. And of course, they remember their neighbors, like Roy Self.

"When I first began to understand names, it was Upshaw, you see. I came to the mill over here when I was a kid just big enough to ride a horse over to where they're tearing that corn up, behind me, you see, to that mill. And I grew up among them. . . . The farms are small, and the people were poor. You see, after the Civil War, the plantations were behind, were broken up and sold in small pieces, small lots. . . . And it was easy to make a living in this country, but it was hard to prosper."

The Upshaws were like their neighbors. They had just enough to get by. They certainly didn't have enough to send Marion Upshaw to college.

"Ten of us graduated from the high
school class. I said, 'I'm going to make it.' They looked around and asked me how. 'You have no money. You have no clothing.' You couldn't get a job washing dishes at that time, because—I mean, there were other people who needed the job worse than you. And for a black man to make it, it was almost impossible. There were no scholarships to be had, no grants, no loans. I'm supposed to be a failure."

But failing was one thing the Upshaws weren't very good at. Marion Upshaw now has three college degrees and is director of services for the entire Nacogdoches school district. And no one knows better than he does that his story is not the story of one person, but part of the story of a family. And a place.

"My generation in another five and ten years will be retiring and they'll be coming back to build houses on this land. This is home. This is where I first discovered the world. I can look across the road where I'm planning to build my home, and see the very spot where I was born. And I hope that in my being there, my children will develop a love for the land, and that they will in the future return to maintain the attitude of family, and to maintain the attitude of kinship. There's a thread that is interwoven throughout the whole, entire family."

Six Flags Over Texas

Six countries have flown their flags over the land we now call Texas. How many of their colors can we still find woven into the fabric of Texas life?

The first thread is really a multi-colored yarn. Spain came into an Indian culture in Texas as well as in Mexico. In both places, the cultures mixed and blended. Today, the strongest evidences of both Indian and Spanish cultures can be seen in the Mexican way of life. Or, to put it more accurately, the Mexican-American way of life.

About 97 percent of the people living in Texas were born in the United States, including most of the people of Mexican origin. The Spanish language, the Mexican fiestas, the Hispanic respect for family and religion and the land—these

A Tigua Indian against the background of the Ysleta Mission in El Paso.

were all part of Texas long before Texas was a part of the United States.

Today, when schools all over the country are struggling with the problems of Spanish-speaking students in an English-speaking system, it is important to remember that Texas once had a school system in which only Spanish was spoken. That was one of the important reasons that American settlers rebelled against Mexican rule.

Treating the Mexican culture in Texas as though it were a foreign influence would be as silly as treating American Indians as though they were foreigners in their own land.

To see the Mexican—or Hispanic—influence on Texas life, you only have to look at the food, the music, the architecture, the art. Or take a handful of city and town names—El Paso, Corpus Christi, San Antonio, San Marcos, Amarillo.

Between the Spanish and Mexican flags, the flag of France flew over Texas. But it didn't last long, and there is not much in Texas today to remind us that it was ever there. And then there was the flag of the Republic of Texas.

You might think that flag was unimportant, too. After all Texas is Texas, whether it's a country or a state. But Texas is the only state in the United States that was a country before it joined the union. And you can still see that in the way Texans feel about their state. There's a certain pride in being a Texan that is almost as strong as the pride in being an American.

The culture of Hispanic peoples in Texas began at the time of the Spanish missions over 300 years ago.

Shelby Scharine

The Republic of Texas came about when colonists in Texas broke away from Mexico. They declared their independence from the Mexican government in much the same way that the original thirteen colonies declared their independence from England. And it was just as important to Texas as that other revolution was to New York and Pennsylvania and Massachusetts. Along with the Boston Tea Party, Paul Revere's Ride, and Washington crossing the Delaware, the people of Texas remember the Alamo.

Next came the flag of the Confederacy. Texas was one of the states that withdrew from the Union during the Civil War. This flag is important because Texas, more than the rest of the

Texas Tourist Development Agency, Photo by Michael Murphy

Southwest, can be called a southern state. These are parts of Texas that have much more in common with Alabama and Missouri than with Arizona and New Mexico. There were once plantations in east Texas. And there were slaves. Texas often votes in national elections the way that the southern states vote. There are shared values and traditions.

The sixth flag over Texas is, of course, the flag of the United States of America. Texas, in the end, is one hundred percent American, not in spite of all those other influences, but because of them. It's the cowboy and the football player, the Indian and the aerospace engineer, the Houston skyscraper and the west Texas cattle range, the poor farmer and the oil-rich millionaire. It's the Hispanic child in the English-speaking school who grows up to become the mayor of San Antonio.

The flags of Texas and the United States . . . San Antonio's mayor, Henry Cisneros . . . and a rodeo parade in Houston.

San Antonio: A Dream of Harmony

San Antonio is a city of differences. Within its boundaries live two cultures, side by side, but not always together.

"We never came out of our neighborhood. I didn't know there were any Anglos. The only Anglos I knew were teachers, and so the only time that we found out there were some other parts of San Antonio is when we took a trip."

Hispanics are the largest minority group in Texas. In San Antonio, they are not a minority. They are the majority. Recently, they became a voting majority, and they helped elect a Mexican-American, Henry Cisneros, mayor of the city.

But for many years, the two cultures of San Antonio had not mixed. Hispanics lived almost entirely in the barrios, low-lying areas that often flooded.

"I remember seeing neighbors having their cars just going down the street, literally. Children losing their lives. It was not unusual."

There were other things that were not unusual in the barrios— poor schools, poverty, poor housing. And a lot of other problems came with those conditions.

"Parents, priests did not like what was happening to the community. People were leaving our communities. People were divorcing. Children were—were not being brought up in the best atmosphere and people were like, at a loss. They felt hopeless. There was beginning to be an increase in crime within our community, a loss of respect for the elderly. That was not what our upbringing had been and so we began to ask the serious questions."

The Hispanic people of San Antonio did more than ask questions. Sonia Hernandez, Beatrice Cortez, and thousands of other Hispanics began to organize. They formed a group called COPS—Communities Organized for Public Service. They registered Hispanic people so they could vote. They got local government to work on the flooding. And education. And housing.

"Where do you start? There is no more start. And so the only thing left is you fight, because you know that if you don't fight . . . you're not teaching your kids to be different than from where you were. You know, maybe we didn't know how, or maybe our parents didn't know how, but we've got to start teaching.

We've got to start teaching now. We cannot afford to let another lifetime go by, another lifetime like this. . . . It's never going to be like this, ever again."

Today things are starting to be very different in San Antonio. Mayor Cisneros sees the city as a model for other places with the same kinds of problems.

"(In San Antonio) you can get nothing done without the support of the larger business community, which tends to be non-Hispanic. You can get nothing done in business that requires major governmental involvement without the inclusion of the Hispanic community. So, the dominant mood in San Antonio today, which makes it different from most cities, is this sense of inclu-sion, participation, and compromise and balance."

And things are not just getting better for the Hispanic community. The entire city has a lot to gain from the Mexican-American culture.

"I think it's good for America at a time when America is becoming in some respects more suburban, more sterile, faster . . . that we would see a culture come into it that respects roots, whose values are religious values, whose personal relationships and family relationships are deep and strong and close to the land and close to the neighborhood. I think that's a positive influence in America."

One can cruise in a barge past the hotels, cafes, and restaurants in San Antonio's River Walk (below).

The Future:
Another Frontier

Texas has always been a frontier state. The people enjoy the challenge of pushing forward into places where no one has ever been. They like breaking new ground.

That may be why Texas, for all its roots in the past, looks with eagerness to the future. For the people of this sprawling state, the future is just one more frontier.

Texas universities are doing research in space medicine. Several corporations design and test space equipment. And of course, there is the Lyndon B. Johnson Space Center, a part of the National Aeronautics and Space Administration. Texas is helping the country push forward into space.

Many national corporations are choosing the large cities of Texas for their homes. In Dallas and Houston, glass and

The Lyndon B. Johnson Space Center in Houston.

Various lifestyles . . . one of the many things that draw people to Texas.

They are drawn by the feeling that Texas is where it's happening. Texas *is* the future.

But Texas has important problems to solve in the years to come. The most important is seeing that all of its people share in the wealth of the land. Texas ranks sixth among all the states in total personal income. But it ranks thirty-third in income per person. In other words, there are quite a few people in Texas who have a lot of money. But there are many, many more who have very little.

When Texas meets this challenge, it will have crossed its most important frontier.

steel office buildings reach high into the sky.

And tens of thousands of people move to Texas every year from other parts of the country.

Important Historical Events in Texas

1519 Alonso Álvarez de Pineda explores the coast of Texas.

1528 Álvar Núñez Cabeza de Vaca and three others are shipwrecked on the Texas coast and later explore parts of the region.

1541 Francisco Vásquez de Coronado passes through west Texas.

1682 Spanish missionaries build the first missions in Texas, near what is today El Paso.

1685 Robert Cavelier, Sieur de la Salle, founds Fort Saint Louis, a French settlement.

1691 Texas becomes a Spanish dominion. A Franciscan friar establishes the first mission in east Texas.

1821 Stephen F. Austin founds American settlements.

1830 Mexico stops Americans from settling in Texas.

1835 The first battle of the Texas revolution takes place.

1836 Texas declares its independence. The Alamo falls to Santa Anna. General Sam Houston captures Santa Anna at the battle of San Jacinto. Texas becomes an independent Republic.

1845 Texas becomes the 28th state on December 29.

1846 War between Mexico and the United States begins.

1861 Texas secedes from the Union.

1865 The last Civil War battle is fought, near Brownsville.

1870 Texas is readmitted to the Union.

1876 The present state constitution is adopted.

1881 The Southern Pacific Railroad links Texas with California.

1901 The Spindletop oil fields are opened south of Beaumont.

1915 The Houston Ship Channel is opened.

1925 Mrs. Miriam A. Ferguson is elected and Texas becomes the second state to have a woman governor.

1952 Dwight D. Eisenhower, born in 1890 in Denison, is elected the 34th president of the United States.

1956 Congress restores Texas tidelands to the state.

1957 A tollway, Texas' first, connecting Dallas and Fort Worth opens.

1963 President John F. Kennedy is assassinated in Dallas.

1964 The Manned Spacecraft Center in the Houston area becomes the headquarters of U.S. astronauts.

1969 Amistad (Friendship) Dam, on the Rio Grande River, is completed—to serve both the U.S. and Mexico.

1978 William P. Clements becomes the first Republican to be elected governor since 1869.

Texas Almanac

Nickname. The Lone Star State.

Capital. Austin.

State Bird. Mockingbird.

State Flower. Bluebonnet.

State Tree. Pecan.

State Motto. Friendship.

State Song. Texas, Our Texas.

State Abbreviations. Tex. (traditional); TX (postal).

Statehood. December 29, 1845, the 28th state.

Government. Congress: U.S. senators, 2; U.S. representatives, 27. **State Legislature:** senators, 31; representatives, 150. **Counties:** 254.

Area. 267,336 sq. mi. (692,397 sq. km.), 2nd in size among the states.

Greatest Distances. north/south, 801 mi. (1,289 km.); east/west, 773 mi. (1,244 km.). **Coastline:** 367 mi. (591 km.)

Elevation. Highest: Guadalupe Peak, 8,751 ft. (2,667 m). **Lowest:** sea level, along Gulf of Mexico.

Population. 1980 Census: 14,228,383 (27% increase over 1970), 3rd among the states; **Density:** 53 persons per sq. mi. (20 persons per sq. km.). **Distribution:** 80% urban, 20% rural. **1970 Census:** 11,198,655.

Economy. Agriculture: beef cattle, cotton. **Fishing Industry:** shrimp. **Manufacturing:** chemicals, nonelectric machinery, and coal products, food products, fabricated metal products, electric machinery and equipment, transportation equipment. **Mining:** petroleum, natural gas, natural gas liquids.

Places to Visit

The Alamo.
Astroworld.
Lyndon B. Johnson Space Center.
Mission San Jose.
Padre Island National Seashore.
San Jacinto Monument.
Six Flags Over Texas, amusement park.

Annual Events

Houston Livestock Show and Rodeo Exposition (February-March).
Texas Independence Day (March 2).
Jefferson Historical Pilgrimage in Jefferson (April-May).
Watermelon Thump in Luling (June).
Aqua Festival in Austin (August).
East Texas Yamboree in Gilmer (October).
Festival of Lights in San Antonio (December).